To John,

Love you always!

From,

Auntie

Cheryl Joanne.

X

QUINTESSENTIAL QUIRKY QUOTES!

CHERYL JOANNE

Published by New Generation Publishing in 2021

First Edition

ISBN   978-1-80369-075-9

www.newgeneration-publishing.com

New Generation Publishing

• QUOTES ARE INTENSELY
IMMEDIATE, THEY KEEP YOU
OBSERVATIONALLY OBEDIENT.

- TIME WILL TELL, THAT'S THE SECRET.

- BE IN CONTROL...FOR IT'S YOUR HAND YOU HOLD.

- THERE IS NO TIME LIKE THE PRESENT DAY, TO ENJOY THE GIFT OF LIFE.

• CONFIDENCE IS THE KEY TO
BEING WHERE YOU WANT TO BE.

• DON'T COMPETE...THIS IS YOUR LIFE TO COMPLETE.

• WE ALL MAKE MISTAKES, JUST DON'T MAKE THE SAME 1 TWICE.

- ANYTHING WORTH DOING IS PRICELESS.

• FOCUS ON THE IMPORTANCE, DON'T REACH OUT FOR RIVALRY REASSURANCE.

• HIGHLIGHT YOUR TWILIGHT, KEEP IT SHINING...KEEP IT BOLDY BRIGHT.

- BE YOUR TRUE ENVY, NOT YOUR ARCH ENEMY.

• IF AT FIRST YOU DON'T SUCCEED...SUCCEED IN TRYING AGAIN.

- 1 RIGHTEOUS RIGHT IS BETTER THAN 2 WRONGFUL WRONGS.

• TRUST YOUR FIRST INSTINCT BY NOT SECOND GUESSING IT.

- JUST BE HAPPY IN YOUR OWN SKIN, THIS IS HOW YOU WILL WISELY WIN.

• ALWAYS HAVE PLAN B, THEN THERE'LL BE BACK UP...YOU'LL SEE.

- I WOULD RATHER STAND ALONE THAN BE UNDIVIDED.

- AS TIME TICKS PRODUCE YOUR TIMELESS TRICKS.

- YOU LEARN TO LIVE, WHEN YOU LIVE TO LEARN.

- IT'S NOT ABOUT BEING RIGHT, IT'S ALL ABOUT GETTING IT RIGHT.

- DON'T TOLERATE THE INTOLERABLE.

- TAKE A BIG STRIDE, KEEP YOUR SMILE BIG & WIDE.

- WHEN YOU TOUCH AT LEAST ONE PERSON'S HEART EACH DAY...THAT'S REMARKABLE IN EVERY-WAY.

- BE YOUR BIGGEST COMPLIMENT, NOT YOUR CRUELLEST CRITIC.

• THINK OF ALL THE GOOD IN YOUR LIFE, NOT THE SADISTIC SAD STRIFE.

• DON'T BE A DAMSEL IN DISTRESS...SETTLE FOR MORE, & NOT FOR ANYTHING LESS.

- KNOWING YOUR WORTH IS
  WONDERFULLY WORTH IT.

- THERE ARE LOTS OF WAYS TO HEAD IN THE RIGHT DIRECTION.

• THE TRUTH CAN HURT, BUT
THAT DOESN'T MEAN YOU SHOULD
HEAL A LIE.

• LOOK INSIDE YOURSELF, &
OUTSIDE WON'T MATTER.

- DON'T GET TOO COMFORTABLE IN WHAT YOU'RE UNCOMFORTABLE DOING.

• WHEN YOU HAVEN'T WORN MY SHOES...DON'T EVEN ATTEMPT TO TRY THEM ON.

- DELIGHTFUL DEDICATION IS THE BEST MENTAL MEDICATION.

- BE KIND TO YOUR MIND...ALLOW IT TO MENTALLY UNWIND.

- YOU CAN DO ANYTHING YOU PUT YOUR MIND TO, WHEN YOU PUT YOUR MIND TO IT.

• SOBRIETY...WHEN ALL THE PIECES OF THE JIGSAW JUST FALL INTO PLACE.

- DON'T DRAIN THE LIFE OUT OF YOUR LIFETIME.

- YOU'VE GOT NOTHING TO LOSE WHEN YOU'VE GOT NOTHING TO GAIN.

- PROOF IS IN THE PERPETUAL PUDDING.

• LESS IS MORE, MORE OR LESS.

- TURN A NEGATIVE INNER THOUGHT INTO A POSITIVE OUTLOOK.

• IT'S ALL ABOUT THE TRANQUIL TIMING, WHEN YOU'RE LOOKING TO VIEW A CLOUD WITH SILVER FINE LINING.

- DON'T ALLOW ANYTHING TO BE TOO EASY, NOR TO TRY TOO HARD.

- PRACTICE WHAT YOU PLAN TO PITCH PERFECT.

• MAKE YOUR OWN
DECISIONS...NO ONE ELSE
DESERVES TO DECIDE.

• DON'T SUGARCOAT SITUATIONS, EVEN IF YOU DO HAVE THE SWEETEST INTENTIONS.

- IT'S ALL ABOUT THE KNOWING, IN ORDER TO KEEP ON GROWING.

- DON'T CUT YOUR NOSE OFF TO SPITE YOUR FORTUNATE SENSE OF SMELL.

- DO SOMETHING UNIQUE EACH DAY, DO IT IN YOUR OWN INDIVIDUAL WAY.

• LET YOUR PAST REFINE YOU...NOT UNDERMINE YOU.

• EVERY EVENT IS EVENTFUL.

- UTILISE YOUR TIME...DON'T ABUSE YOUR TIME.

• TO TURN THE CORRECT CORNER YOU MUST USE THE RIGHT ANGLE.

- YOU DON'T NEED TO BE PERFECT
  TO BE PERFECTLY PRECISE.

- DON'T CHEAPEN WHAT YOU VALUE.

- THE ONLY TIME YOU WASTE IS THE TIME YOU ARE WASTING.

- EVERY IMPROVEMENT DESERVES APPROVAL.

- WHERE THERE IS CLARITY THERE IS SOUND SANITY.

- REMAIN CALM...THIS CAUSES LESS HARM.

- LIFE IS ABOUT CHOICES, DON'T CHOOSE TO BE LEFT WITHOUT ANY.

- GET ON WITH YOUR DESTINED DAY...NEVER ALLOW ANYONE TO STAND IN YOUR WAY.

- DON'T BE A WALLFLOWER,
  BLOOM BY THE HOUR.

• PROTECT YOURSELF...THERE IS NO BETTER BODY ARMOUR.

• FLOURISH & GROW, DON'T JUST GO WITH THE FLOW.

• KEEP DOING YOU...YOUR AUTHENTIC SELF KNOWS WHAT TO DO.

- TO BE SURE OF BEING SURE, REVIEW THE SUBJECT FURTHERMORE.

• THE BLAMING GAME IS ONLY PLAYED BY PEOPLE WHO ARE FULL OF SHAME.

• BE YOUR OWN BEST
FRIEND...YOU'LL HAVE ETERNAL
FRIENDSHIP RIGHT TO THE END.

- IN ORDER TO APPRECIATE THE GOOD YOU MUST DEPRECIATE THE BAD.

- YOU OWE IT TO YOURSELF TO PAY FOR A GREAT LIFE.

• REMEMBER NOT TO FORGET
WHAT YOU'VE ALREADY GOT.

- THE LEG WORK SPEAKS LOUDER THAN THE TONGUE WORK.

• FIND YOUR GLOWING GIFT...GIVE YOURSELF A LOVELY LIFT.

• NEVER ALLOW ANYONE'S
THOUGHTS TO DETERMINE
YOUR'S.

• TO SEE IT IS TO BELIEVE IT, BUT YOU MUST FEEL WHAT YOU TRULY BELIEVE.

- WHEN CRITICAL COMMENTS ARE SAID...DON'T ALLOW THEM TO ENTER YOUR HEAD.

- YOU GET BACK WHAT YOU PUT FORWARD.

- LAUGH OUT LOUD AT THE IRRATIONAL CROWD.

- ONE POSITIVE PROJECT EACH DAY, WILL HELP TO KEEP NEGATIVITY AT BAY.

- SPREAD YOUR LASTING LOVE,
LIKE THE WINGS OF A WHITE
TURTLE DOVE.

- DON'T CHANGE YOUR WAY
WHEN OTHERS HAVE THEIR SAY.

- THE THOUGHT IS OFTEN WORSE THAN THE DEED...THINKING WHERE THE DEED COULD LEAD.

- BE YOUR PERSONAL BEST, GET BACK YOUR SENSATIONAL ZEST.

- KNOW THAT YOUR LIMITS ARE LIMITLESS.

- BEING SELF SUFFICIENT WILL MAKE YOU MORE EFFICIENT.

• YOU CAN RUIN A REPUTATION
WITH JUST ONE ACCUSATION.

- MAKE YOURSELF AN OATH TO CHOOSE PERSONAL GROWTH.

- SET THE BAR TO WHERE YOU ARE.

- CORRECT IT...DON'T ERRATICALLY INSPECT IT.

• IT'S ALL ABOUT
ATTITUDE...CHOOSE MINDFUL
GRATITUDE.

- WHEN LOVE RUNS DRY, DON'T DRY IT OUT.

• LET GO OF YESTERDAY, &
INVITE IN TOMORROW FOR
COME WHAT MAY.

• BE YOUR OWN RESCUE
REMEDY...LISTEN TO THAT
MAGICAL MELODY.

• DON'T HAVE TIME ON YOUR
HANDS WHEN OPPORTUNITIES ARE
AT YOUR VERY FINGERTIPS.

- IT'S ONLY MORALLY RIGHT TO APOLOGISE WHEN YOU'RE REALISTICALLY WRONG.

• DON'T PUT YOURSELF ON THE
BACK BURNER...GET OUT THERE &
BE A HEAD TURNER.

• YOU'RE HERE TO MAKE A CHANGE NOT RUTHLESSLY REARRANGE.

• GIVE YOURSELF A BLISSFUL
BREAK FOR GOODNESS SAKE.

• LIVE LIKE NO ONE IS LOOKING.

- SHOW AN INTEREST IN WHAT YOU'RE INTERESTED IN.

- DANCE LIKE YOU HAVE THE WORLD UNDER YOUR FEET.

- EXERCISE WHAT YOU VERBALISE.

- DON'T GET EVEN JUST GET BETTER.

- TEACH YOURSELF HOW YOU WOULD LIKE TO BE TAUGHT.

- WHEN IN DOUBT BE
  DOUBTFUL.

- YOU CAN ONLY ACTIVELY ACHIEVE.

• DON'T LOOK BACK WHILST
YOU'RE MOVING FORWARD, AS
YOU'LL RISK FALLING OVER.

- ACCIDENTS DON'T PURPOSELY HAPPEN.

• BE GRATEFUL FOR ALL THAT
YOU HAVE, & YOU'LL HAVE ALL
THAT YOU'RE GRATEFUL FOR.

- SLIDING DOORS CAN ONLY OCCUR WHEN YOUR DOORS ARE LEFT OPEN.

- BE EMPOWERED BY THE SWEET NOT THE SOURED.

- KEEP IT SIMPLISTIC...KEEP IT REALISTIC.

- SOULFULLY STRIVE, DON'T JUST BE AMICABLY ALIVE.

- LIFE CAN BE ASTOUNDING
WITH THE SUITABLE
SURROUNDING.

- CLOSE YOUR PAST DOOR...ENABLE YOUR FUTURE DOOR TO ALLURE.

- WHAT YOU REGRETTED NOT DOING COULD BE THE BEST THING YOU EVER DIDN'T DO.

- REVIEW EVERYTHING YOU SEE, DON'T JUST VIEW HOW YOU WOULD LIKE THINGS TO BE.

- HELP YOUR MIND PRODUCE A POSITIVE PERSPECTIVE...NOT AN OPEN OBJECTIVE.

- WHEN KNOW WHO YOU ARE,
  YOU'VE COME SO FAR.

- EXPLAIN YOURSELF TO YOU...NOT TO OTHERS, WHEN THEY ASK YOU TO.

• YOU WILL NEVER GET A SECOND CHANCE AT A FIRST IMPRESSION.

- ENROL IN A GOAL.

- BE INFLUENCED BY THE INFLUENTIAL.

• STAND UP FOR YOURSELF...YOU WON'T GET ANYWHERE SITTING DOWN.

- KEEP YOURSELF PHYSICALLY FIT, YOU'LL FEEL STRONGER AFTER 1 HOURLY HIT.

- PERFECTLY PRACTICE WHAT YOU PREDOMINANTLY PREACH.

- EXPOSE YOUR PRIDE WHEN YOU'VE NOTHING TO HIDE.

- ACKNOWLEDGE YOUR
  KNOWLEDGE.

- HAVING EVERYTHING UNDER CONTROL, IS SO OVERRATED.

• BE AHEAD OF YOUR GAME...CARRY AN UMBRELLA WHEN IT'S FORECAST RAIN.

- DON'T TOLERATE THE INTOLERABLE.

• GET LOST IN THE MOMENT...DON'T LET THE MOMENT LOSE YOU.

- YOU CAN ONLY JUSTIFY THE JUSTIFIABLE.

• FIND A POSITIVE IN EVERYTHING...EVEN RUBBISH CAN BE RECYCLED.

- DETERMINE YOUR DETERMINATION.

• RELY ON YOURSELF TO NOT LET
YOURSELF DOWN.

- WORK HARD AT WORKING HARDER.

- SOMETHING LIFE CHANGING CAN ONLY HAPPEN WHEN YOU CHANGE YOUR LIFE.

- PURSUE WHAT YOU'RE PURSUING.

• BEING SELF SATISFIED WILL
FILL YOU WITH BEAMING PRIDE.

• YOUR JOURNEY CAN BE
JOYOUS WHEN YOU'RE FEELING
JOYFUL.

• YOU CAN ONLY GET TO THE BOTTOM OF WHAT YOU BEGIN.

- FIND A PASSION THAT WILL NEVER GO OUT OF FASHION.

- BE CLEVER ABOUT BEING CORRECT.

• FIND YOUR FORTE.

• YOU CAN'T CONTROL THE
ACTIONS OF OTHERS, BUT YOU
CAN CONTROL YOUR REACTIONS
TO THEM.

• DON'T WORRY ABOUT WHAT
ANYONE THINKS...THEY'VE GOT
THEIR OWN PROBLEMS TO
WORRY ABOUT.

- ONLY YOU CAN ONLY STAND ON YOUR OWN TWO FEET.

- YOUR PRIORITIES LIE WITH WHAT YOU PRIORITISE.

• SELF LOVE IS THE BEST GIFT
THAT YOU WILL EVER RECEIVE.

- NEVER NEGLECT YOUR SELF RESPECT.

- YOU CAN CREATE A QUOTE THAT'S MIND BLOWING, IT'S ALL ABOUT...INSPIRATIONAL KNOWING.

CHERYL JOANNE WAS BORN IN LIVERPOOL, UK. SHE BEGAN WRITING POWERFUL WORDS OF WISDOM, AFTER OVERCOMING HER ALCOHOL ADDICTION IN MARCH 2020; RESULTING IN A TRUE SOBRIETY SUCCESS STORY. SHE IS DEDICATING THIS BOOK TO HER RECOVERY.

Milton Keynes UK
Ingram Content Group UK Ltd.
UKHW010120280923
429506UK00002B/2

9 781803 690759